GraniteLand

'Leave nothing but footprints, take away only memories.'

Published in 2004 by Compass Rose Publishing

ISBN 0-9547332-0-7

British Library Cataloguing-in-Publication Data – A catalogue record for this book
is available from the British Library.

Copyright Jenny Leathes 2004

Printed in Great Britain by R. Booth Ltd., Antron Hill, Mabe, Penryn, Cornwall TR10 9HH

All photographs in this book are available as limited edition archival ink jet prints.

Please contact the author via her website: www.compassrosephotography.co.uk

GraniteLand

A journey along the Tinner's Way, an ancient track in Penwith, West Cornwall, focusing on the 'moorstone' of this Celtic landscape.

The photographs are a personal response to the distinctive stone features of this unique county.

The words place the granite in context, combining my own reactions with geology, history, the natural elements and the workings of mankind.

Jenny Leathes

The Tinner's Way

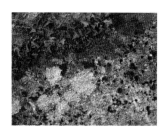

Grid references (SW351318) are marked on the top left hand corner on relevant pages. Ordnance Survey Explorer Map 102 Lands End was used.

Foreword

Granite was such a natural part of the Cornish landscape I grew up in that my reaction to this wonderful rock was to spend what seems most of my life clambering over it and researching its properties and uses. Granite is, quite literally, the backbone of Cornwall from Bodmin Moor to the very tip of Land's End. This ancient igneous rock was intruded beneath a mountain chain of older rocks 290 million years ago and slowly cooled before the forces of erosion and weathering exposed it in geologically recent times. West Penwith has the coarsest granite, exhibiting rough crystals of quartz and feldspar interspersed with sparkling mica and some black tourmaline, the whole mix often discoloured by other minerals.

Granite is ever present here, in grand sea cliffs, scattered rocks or wild moorlands, where man's works are granite too, for this is a landscape steeped in prehistory, with tiny stone-walled fields, and a place ravaged by tin and copper mining. There is something about the enduring granite, so full of texture, which makes this western land so timeless and very special. Artists and writers have responded to the granite's remarkable brooding presence, and to some the rock seems almost alive (remember, it was once molten). Such feelings are not easy to pin down, yet Jenny Leathes has achieved this through her sensitive photography.

These striking and very beautiful images portray a vision of a truly granite landscape seen through the eyes of a photographer. Jenny's photographs capture perfectly the beauty and texture of the ancient stone. The close studies are chosen with care for their intimate detail, while atmospheric skies hang over the wider landscape views. Her captions are based on personal observations, and she goes for what interests her. In these few pages Jenny Leathes has caught the very essence of the granite of Cornwall's far west, and there is a promise of so much more as she takes us along the Tinner's Way from Cape Cornwall to St Ives.

Peter Stanier

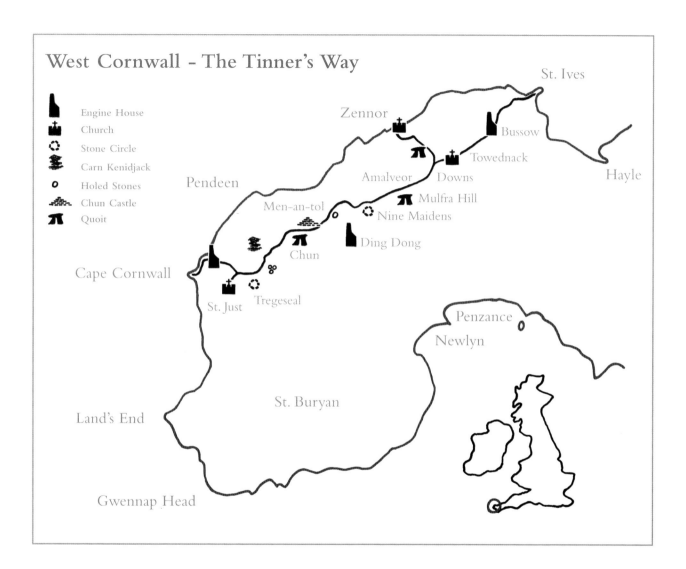

West Cornwall - The Tinner's Way

Legend:
- Engine House
- Church
- Stone Circle
- Carn Kenidjack
- Holed Stones
- Chun Castle
- Quoit

St. Ives

Zennor

Bussow

Towednack

Amalveor

Downs

Pendeen

Mulfra Hill

Hayle

Men-an-tol

Nine Maidens

Ding Dong

Chun

Cape Cornwall

Tregeseal

St. Just

Penzance

Newlyn

St. Buryan

Land's End

Gwennap Head

Cape Cornwall

The Cape

This noble promontory stands alone completely exposed to the Atlantic storms. It is composed of slate rock traversed by granite veins. On top stands a striking chimney, a remnant of the tin mining industry, which originally served the boiler of a beam winder. On a clear day, about twenty miles away across the buried land of Lyonesse, the Scilly Isles are just visible. Nearer, Land's End can be seen, and the treacherous rocks of Longships lie off the dramatic granite cliffs. Either side of the Cape lie Priest's Cove and Porthledden Cove.

Priest's Cove

A few local fishing boats sit on the steep, short slipway below old sheds, cobbled together from lumps of granite, slate and concrete. A hundred years ago boats would weave out between the rocks to go and catch the large shoals of pilchards. The Brisons, a set of jagged rocks, home to many birds, stand clear for all to see. Centuries ago these rocks were known as the Brissens, meaning prisons, and were in fact used to hold criminals. Needless to say below the surface lie many wrecks and in the past locals have benefited from salvaging much booty. Perhaps the most unusual was the British Submarine L1: she broke adrift from her tug whilst being towed to Newport after the First World War.

Watching the autumn sun dip down behind the horizon, seabirds land on the jagged Brisons. There is a captivating stillness punctured by the sound of crashing waves on the rocks. Another day has gone and life around the Cape is plunged into semi-darkness.

Cornish
Porthledden: Wide Cove

Porthledden Cove

Going down into the corner of the cove, one comes across huge egg shapes: granite boulders worn round and smooth, sitting on a rock base. It's surreal and somehow quite symbolic. Many eggs are massive textured shapes of great strength. The sea crashes in and rolls them about wearing them down. The eggs are symbolic of beginning, like the start of this journey, yet they are so ancient. They are witnesses to the passage of time, millions of years, and have no connection with mankind, except some people try to remove them and this is unlawful.

The granite eggs are the result of many thousands of years of erosion and climate change, with sea levels rising and falling. Even today the process continues; at Porth Nanven, the next cove south of the Cape, boulders from a raised beach still fall into the sea and the rolling and smoothing continues.

The granite eggs speak of life and the passing of ages. I am here for just a fleeting moment.

Cornish
Porth Nanven: The white cove
Porthledden Cove was known as Port Caniack: cove/landing place for Kenidjack hamlet

Kenidjack Valley

The Porthledden rock bed is slate, but granite and other minerals integrate with it. I am captivated by these little pockets of varying colour and texture. Moving on along this cove I scramble over huge coarse granite blocks that have fallen out of the cliffs, hiding rock pools. At the other end of this 150 metre cove there are small granite pebbles that I can pick up; the colour and texture has changed. A stream tumbles down a narrow valley from the Bostraze moors, I am standing where it reaches the sea. In days gone by it played a significant role, powering water wheels to mill corn and work stamps for crushing tin ore. One of the wheels was reputedly the largest in the county, nearly twenty metres in diameter.

This valley and stream has a number of names: Nancherrow, Boswedden, Tregeseal or Kenidjack. It is littered with old mining remains. The small tin, copper and arsenic mines became known as Boswedden and Wheal Castle. A restored wheel pit sits above the cove. This area is part of the mining district of St. Just, a town just inland of this valley, known as the capital of the industry. It was probably the main starting point, centuries ago, for the transporting of tin, on mules across the moors.

Other minerals contrast with the granite; here, the lodes of tin ore are visible. The images are about the variety of colour and texture, the feeling of preciousness in the stone and the value of being alive today. For me there is an atmosphere of loss and decay here, echoes of a vanished industrial past.

Cornish
Kenidjack: fuel ground
Boswedden: white dwelling
Nan: valley
Wheal: mine

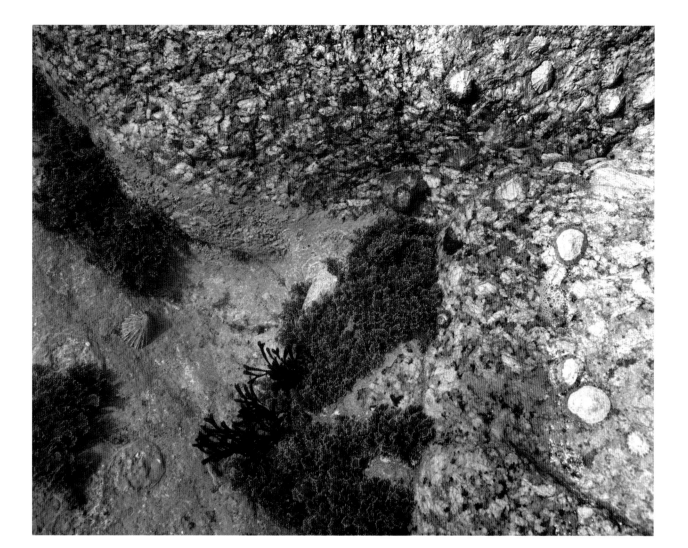

Wheal Owles and Wheal Edward

Wandering along the coastal path to the next mining area, one passes by the Iron Age Kenidjack castle and old rifle butts high up on the cliffs. The edge of this granite land is pierced by a number of deep gullies known as 'Zawns': Buzz and Gen, South Zawn, North Zawn and Wheal Edward Zawn.

Wheal Owles and Wheal Edward, standing high beside the Tinner's path, are the restored remains of engine houses from the tin industry. Today the typical engine house is widely used as a symbol of Cornwall and all things Cornish, from industrial heritage to locally produced food and cycle paths.

The tin and copper ores are found in veins or lodes in high concentrations. The lodes tend to occur alongside vertical sheets of surrounding granite rock. Where the outcrops occurred in the cliffs the sea eroded the softer rock between the granite creating 'zawns'. During the Bronze Age this tin and copper were easily accessible and used to make tools and weapons. Wheal Edward was also known for its uranium and today exploration is seriously discouraged due to the high levels of radiation. Wheal Owles had a sad ending; nineteen men and a boy were lost in 1893 due to flooding. The bodies have never been recovered.

A variety of minerals can be found in the granite that makes up the field walls, engine houses and spoil heaps. The heaps reveal little plant life, probably due to the toxic presence of arsenic.

My images are the remains of today, the signs of history and hints at man's livelihood.

Cornish
Wheal Owles: cliff mine
Zawn: cleft in cliffs
Zawn Buzz and Gen: chasm by the giant's dwelling

So that es the awful story of the floodin' of Wheal Owles,

Thas 'ow the blinds are lowered and the Church-bell sadly tolls;

The mine is now a grave-yard, and the levels are the graves,

And the miners' dust there slumbers near the wild Atlantic waves!

W. Herbert Thomas 1893

Carn Kenidjack

Leaving the coast behind, one now heads east for the high West Penwith moors, up onto Truthwall and Botallack Common.

Carn Kenidjack stands boldly alone on top of the moors, surrounded by common land known as the 'Gump' which holds many clues to its historical past. Sitting on top of this magnificent, irregular layered granite tor one can see for miles across the Penwith Peninsula and out to sea; a good place to let one's mind wander. The breeze on the outcrop creates some gentle whistling noises, giving rise to the name the 'Hooting Carn'. The Gump is bleak. Amongst the heather and gorse, a number of tumuli and granite stones including some holed ones can be found. Not too far away stands the Tregeseal stone circle.

A feeling of mysteriousness and spiritual connection to the past reigns here. One is walking across a funerary landscape, a surface covered in old, tough vegetation; from time to time the moorland fires scorch it all black. The granite survives and continues its long witness.

Legends abound: fairy stories of little people making harmonious music, dancing or leading a benighted traveller astray. Lost souls who wandered across the moor at night found themselves fought back by demons at a stile or pursued by the resident fiend, a shadowy form with a lantern, riding a half-starved pony. Witches assembled and cast their spells. Travelling across the Gump, particularly at night, left many travellers trembling with fear.

Cornish
Penwith: promontory of blood!
Botallack: Talek's big/heavy dwelling
Gump: downs

The Tregeseal Stone Circle

This granite circle lies south of Carn Kenidjack, on the lower slopes of Truthwall common. It is the only survivor of three prehistoric stone circles in this area. In recent years it has been restored and now contains nineteen upright stones. Conjecture remains as to the purpose of these circles but it is believed they were used for rituals or ceremonies. This circle lies near tumuli, stone age burial areas, which may indicate a link between the two.

Stone Circles

Stone circles began to appear after about 2500 BC in Penwith. The stones often surrounded barrows and they were carefully placed in alignment with the sun, moon, stars or other distant stones and structures.

Holed Stones

Standing in a line are three granite stones each with a small hole, about the size of a fist. Another stone has fallen over and the fifth once broke in half, but has since been joined together and now stands again. They may be very ancient and no one really knows what they were used for; just another mystery to the place.

Cornish
Carn: rock pile
Tregeseal: Catihael's farm

Chun Castle

Crossing Woon Gumpus Common and walking up onto the top of the hill one passes the ancient cromlech known as Chun Quoit. On the summit, 215 metres above sea level, stands a well preserved Iron Age hill fort. It was built in the third century BC and made entirely of small granite rocks, moorstones gathered from the surrounding land. Some of the massive inner and outer circular walls still exist. The fort is over sixty metres in diameter. The remaining parts in some places stand nearly two metres high and one and a half metres wide. On the west side stands the entrance. Inside, in what is known as the courtyard, one can still see a stone-lined well. This hill fort, apart from protecting people and livestock, may have been used for storing and smelting the precious tin ore, an important commodity in the economy of Penwith. Sadly, the past few centuries have seen some of the granite rocks taken for local buildings in Madron and pavements in Penzance.

Cornish
Woon Gumpus: level downs
Chun: house on downland
Madron: derived from the church of Saint Madern
Penzance: holy headland

Chun Quoit

This is an early Neolithic chambered tomb which lies on barren moorland just below the summit. It stands nearly two metres high in a box-shaped, mushroom-like form with four upright granite slabs, three of which support a large capstone. Like other quoits in the area it may have been buried with possibly the capstone revealed, or used as a venue for ceremonial and ritual purposes. It stood here for two thousand years before the fort was built, and still survives now. This ancient structure commands much respect.

The high spacious plateau gives extensive views out over the Atlantic. One looks across this ancient moor where the strength of granite has been used for centuries; in pre-historic settlements, Cornish hedges and more modern buildings. Some hefty cattle move about minding their own business and the leftover daffodils are dying down after the spring crop. People are still trying to make a living out of this unforgiving barren landscape.

Bosullow Trehyllys Settlement

Bosullow, an ancient village, sits on the flat below the north-east slope of Chun Castle. Remains of low, granite domestic enclosures exist within field systems separated by drystone hedges, also of granite.

The Cornish Hedge

Cornish hedges are made from granite boulders and smaller stones with or without earth bank faces. They are a distinctive style to the county. Both hedge types exist along the Way and vary in style and age. The dry types exist in abundance on the high moor probably due to the large quantities of moorstone lying on the ground and the shallow soil. Enclosures are believed to have originated in the Neolithic period. Real settlements began when the Celts arrived from Brittany in the Bronze Age, when small field systems were marked out adjacent to the settlement. The land was cleared and the granite stones piled up to create banks. Granite slabs were dragged in to form the enclosure, smaller stones filled the gaps.

Walls here at Bosullow and at Bodrifty, further along the Way, are thought to belong to ancient times. Photographing the hedges and settlements gives me a feeling for their long history, time moving on through many centuries. Man's presence is evident, but from long ago.

Cornish
Bosullow: dwelling by house of light
Bos, Bod: dwelling

Boskednan Moor

I am high on the moor, absorbing my surroundings while I sit on a fallen granite stone, eating my lunch. I notice soaring buzzards and a distant raven tumbling in the air currents. One can sit here and take in many features of the Way. Looking back south-westerly, the strange profile of Carn Kenidjack is nearly five miles away. Nearer lies Bosullow Common and its working and derelict farms, distinctive granite Cornish hedges and stiles; strange ceremonial or ritual stones are closer by. Just to the north-west stand the impressive granite hills of Carn Galver and Hannibals Carn. Both the north and south Cornish coasts can be clearly seen.

Nine Maidens stone circle

Over two hundred metres above sea level, this circle is laid out on a saddle looking over two natural basins of land. It seems this circle was intended to be part of the landscape rather than dominate it. There are five upright and other fallen or severely leaning granite stones. To me, this is a place where one can pause and admire the views.

Cornish
Boskednan: dwelling of reeds

The Men-an-Tol

The meaning of this name is 'holed stone', and that is exactly what it is, with two upright stones either side. This is one of the most visited sites in Penwith. It is possible to crawl through the hole. Folk believed the stone had healing and fertility properties; it was said to cure children of rickets if they crawled through nine times facing the sun. I feel this site is so vulnerable, I hope the holed stone does not fall over due to over-use by energetic visitors. To put a fence around it, like Stonehenge, would be very sad.

The Mên Scryfa Menhir

A two metre high granite stone stands in the middle of a field and bears an inscription RIALOBRAN - CUNOVAL - FIL, meaning Royal Raven, son of a famous leader. The stone's name means 'stone of writing'. The menhir was probably erected during the Bronze Age and was inscribed in another era, 5th/6th century AD, in a Latinised form of the Celtic language. The legend tells of a warrior son, Rialobran, who wanted to regain his father's lands from a foreigner. During a hard fought single combat Rialobran was killed. He was buried under this stone. The black raven was a symbol of military victory, associated with battles and death.

Cornish
Menhir: long stone

"Lo! on a narrow neck of land

Twixt two unbounded seas I stand,

Secure, insensible,

A point of time, – a moments space, –

Removes me to that heavenly place,

Or shuts me up in hell."

John Wesley 1759

Ding Dong Mine

Looking south from Boskednan moor this distinctive engine house stands proud. I cannot help but mention it as it dominates the skyline for good part of the walk, from Chun to Mulfra Hill.

Photographs in this area record the use of granite in various forms: as ancient monuments, in a derelict house, stuffed in a bank or built into the magnificent walls. A sense of history and the spirit of Cornish generations just dominates this place.

Bodrifty Settlement

On the western slopes of Mulfra Hill one walks through a wonderful example of a Bronze and Iron Age village. Walls, earthworks and hut circles can be seen clearly in this remote granite settlement. There are a few stunted windswept trees and wandering livestock frequent the area.

Mulfra Hill

The path takes one north-east over the lower part of the hill clearly marked by parish boundary stones. The local buzzard has used one for a perch to eat a vole, leaving the bony, bloody remains behind. Rocks are scattered about all over the hill, still some left over after the centuries of settlement building. Further east, just a little way from the summit is Mulfra Quoit. This ancient burial chamber stands approximately three metres high. Its huge granite capstone, weighing around five tonnes, overlooks Mount's Bay. It is worth the detour to have a look. My last visit was in the winter snow.

Cornish
Mulfra: bare domed hill

Amalveor Downs

Walking along the road and track through Kerrowe, I am struck by some wonderful, old, impregnable granite cottages and working farms. Cornish hedges are all around, but with a different style and feel to them, probably younger too. Arriving on these downs, the path divides: towards Zennor, or to Towednack and then St. Ives. I have taken both paths on other days and each are linked to the Tinner's Way.

Cornish
Amalveor: great hill slope
Kerrowe: stags valley
Zennor: after St. Senara to whom the church is dedicated

Zennor Hill

It stands 230 metres high crowned with huge layered granite outcrops. A steep north-westerly slope covered in rock plunges down to the village of Zennor and out towards the cliffs.
In the past this area has provided granite for local buildings from a quarry. Further below is a spider's web of walls from one farm to the next. The huge expanse of the Atlantic sea and sky dominates the view for miles and miles. For me the atmosphere of the moorland journey is ending. The peace and space up here are shortly to be left behind. It is not suprising artists have been deeply influenced by this landscape. The building known as the Carne on this hill has been home to a few. It is remote, no road to it, just a track. Gales and storms have left their mark. Some of the granite outcrops have been given names: the 'Logan Stone' and the 'Polar Bear.'

Zennor Quoit

Before reaching the final tops of Zennor Hill one passes the largest Neolithic cromlech in Penwith, positioned on this high moor looking out to sea. This granite tomb is also known as a portal dolmen because it has an additional front chamber and an outer entrance. It was probably built five to six thousand years ago. Part of it has collapsed; the capstone weighing over nine tonnes has slipped, resting at an angle.

Cornish
Carne: rock pile
Logan: balance

LOGAN-STONE

if it were one
stone it would not be magical
if it were two stones the attrition of
rain cutting into its natural weakness too well
it would not be magical if its massif could be set
trembling neither two nor one for a moment only say
the logging-point of night-fall it would be magical yet
not miraculous small worlds may be born of such magic
but that it can go on and on without ceasing dazzling
the spectator with immobile motion neither two nor one
neither one or two doomed and unshakable on its point
of infinity that is the miracle to be so weak
a finger logs it what constant strength
what force it takes to be a
logan-
stone you and I what cold applied
granite-fire logging on weakness no storm can move us

D. M. Thomas 1971

The village of Zennor

A small, ruggedly-built granite church, a farm and pub dominate this tiny windswept place of great Cornish character. Behind the farm and village houses, hidden away in boulders and brambles, is the 'Giant's Rock'. This is an enormous oval granite boulder with several scooped out curved shapes, ideal for sitting in providing there are no rain puddles!

The church of St. Senara stands raised above the road. It dates from Norman times and probably stands on the site of a 6th century Celtic church. It is possibly named after a Breton Priestess, a Celtic neighbour across the channel. Though this building is rooted in the past, it is far more recent than many places found on the moor. Granite surpasses time.

It is difficult to believe that fishermen once set out from a coastline as harsh as this one, with no obvious safe havens. A legend involving a mermaid (Cornish 'Morveren') and a local chorister is recalled by carvings on the medieval bench-ends in the church.

The photographs here are about light and its effect on the ancient stone. I am fascinated by the way man has shaped the granite to build this church. Sunlight passing through the windows leaving small patches of coloured light on the mouldy walls.

I find Zennor strange and fascinating, I am not sure why. Probably the name; it conjures up a magical feeling of intrigue. It is the one place I have heard Cornish spoken, on a Sunday morning when people were going to a church service.

Towednack

Coming down off the high moor towards St Ives we enter mining country again.
Towednack church is at the centre of this parish, which formerly boasted more than 20 tin
mines, the final closure taking place in 1923. Now derelict engine houses are mute reminders
of a once thriving industry. The chancel arch in the church dates from the 14th century.
A granite altar slab and the roughly circular churchyard suggest much earlier origins.
Once again granite predominates in the church and nearby farm buildings.

Churches like this seem full of history, filtering the past as sunlight is filtered through stained
glass windows. Light, in my eyes, represents life. It has been seen as the symbol of God's
illuminating grace and strength – the light of the world. Finding my own light gives me an
aim on which to focus during times of emotional stress.

Cornish
Towednack: after St Winwalo the patron of the church

Bussow

Across the fields of Chytodden we reach the mining area of Bussow. In 1861 it became known as Tyringham Consols, producing copper and black tin for another ten years.
The walls hold some fascinating stones, unearthed by the mining activities of the past.

Near Bussow farm, but not visible from this path, stands a 13th century granite culver house or dove-cote. It is round with a domed beehive roof and was for breeding pigeons which were a source of meat. There are holes in the wall for access. The farm tenants fed the birds with their grain and the local lord ate them!

Stennack

Walking along the minor roads we enter the outlying area of St. Ives, known as Stennack. It was an important productive mining area for many centuries and at its busiest was known as St. Ives Consols. In 1894 the Stennack river rose, damaging some houses and during 2002 shops in St. Ives were flooded. In 1920 Bernard Leach set up his pottery here which today is still in use.

The atmosphere of this walk is rapidly changing. The ragged edges of the outskirts of St. Ives are full of the signs of 21st century living. I wake up from a dream walking on tarmac.
The signs of the mining past are vitually non-existent. The roads are busy, I have to avoid the traffic. I pass compact housing and bed and breakfast land, until I glimpse the beauty of Porthmeor. The breaking surf, sunlight on the sea and sand. A strong contrast which fires my imagination once more.

Cornish
Stennack: 'Place of Tin'
Porthmeor: great cove.

St. Ives

Walking along the Tinner's Way one understands why so many artists have been drawn to the area and deeply inspired. St Ives has become a centre for artists and an important area for the development of British art particularly in the early 20th century. Entering St. Ives, thoughts of high, wide open spaces give way to the bustle of the 21st century. The small, compact, granite town is built around a semi-circular harbour, protected from the open sea by a granite pier. Almost entirely surrounded by sea, St. Ives is full of light.

St Ives was originally called Porth Ia after an Irish saint who came to Cornwall between the 5th and 7th centuries. She was highly respected and seen as a protector of the fishermen: St Ives was built on the success of fishing. During the tin mining era the town was surrounded by a busy industry. Granite houses and Smeaton's Pier dominate the harbour. The pier was built under the guidance of John Smeaton in the 18th century; it protects the town with a long curve, creating a sheltered pool for the fishing fleets. Walking around the bottom of the pier at low water one can see huge granite blocks in a very thick wall. As one steps onto the pier there are three arches underneath; these were built to allow the current to prevent sand accumulating in the harbour. Two lighthouses rise from the pier, one granite and the other made of cast iron.

The granite images taken here relate to the declining fishing industry in what is now a tourist town. The bottom of the pier traps rubbish, weed, rusting iron, dead fish and old crab shells. The footprints of scavenging seagulls are visible in the sand.

At the end of my journey the last impression is of decay - the fragility of living things and human aspirations. The granite endures.

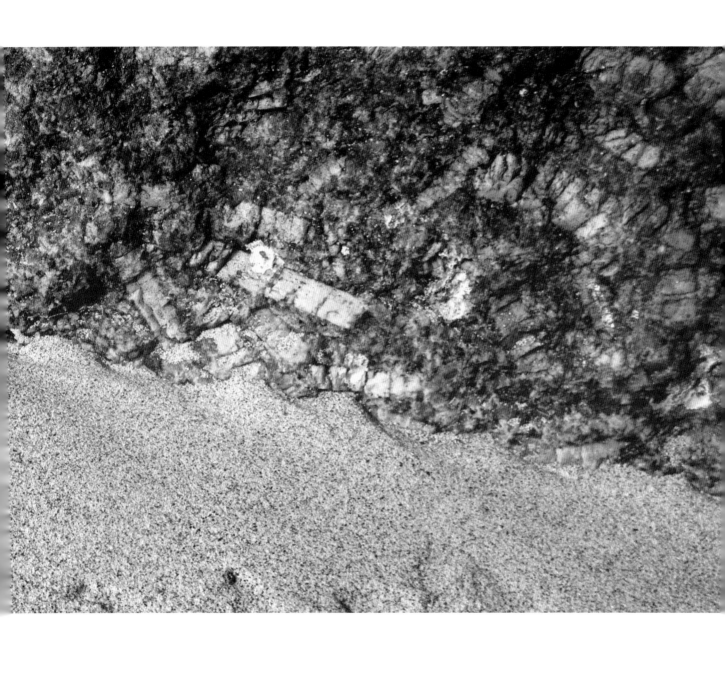

’Tis well! Cornubia’s rich and varied views

Have long employ’d and gratified the Muse,

And what, by Art or Nature here is stor’d,

Her eye, not inattentive, hath explor’d,

Homeward my steps I bend, with bounding heart,

The wand’rings of the Minstrel to impart.

George Woodley 1819

Jenny Leathes

Jenny was born in Hampshire and her journey through life has brought her to Cornwall. She has lived here for 20 years and is passionate about the Cornish landscape, especially the wild and lonely places.

She originally trained as a potter, and continues to enjoy the arts and outdoor education through working with young people.

Photography allows her to explore the land in her own personal way. Her own experiences are at the core of her art work. She focuses on documenting subjects in the landscape in a way that reveals their history, their links with humanity and the effects of the natural elements.

The granite she has chosen to photograph is beautiful, strong and very ancient. It offers a stark contrast to our own short, often fragile but very precious lives.

Peter Stanier

Dr. Peter Stanier was born and brought up in Liskeard. He now lives away from Cornwall in Dorset where he lectures and writes on archaeology, industrial archaeology and landscapes. A one-time rock climber, keenly interested in archaeology and geology, he has researched and published a number of books and papers on the Cornish mining and quarrying industries. Granite is his life-long specialism and his well received book *South West Granite* is the authoritative account of the quarrying industry in Cornwall and Devon.

Acknowledgements

I would like to thank the following, in no particular order, for all their help, encouragement and support in helping me publish this book.

The Tutors at Falmouth College of Arts in particular, Dr. Daro Montag, Kate Lithgow and Colin Jacobson.

Laurence Sutherland for guidance with graphic design.

Peter Larner and Annabel Leathes for proof reading and helping me put into words what I really wanted to say.

Eddie Ephraums for giving me a week's insight into the publication world.

The staff at the Cornish Studies Library, Alma Place, Redruth who helped me with my researches.

My parents for funding my final unit of a Master of Art's programme that led to this publication.

The use of the Logan Stone poem published in The Puberty Tree: Selected Poems is by the kind permission of the author, D. M. Thomas.

Ivan Corbett of Tormark book distributors for his time and advice.

Ordnance Survey for the use of 1908 OS Map St. Ives Sheet – LXI NE & SE "© Crown Copyright 1908" and 1906 OS Map Cape Cornwall – LXXIII NE & LXXIII NW "© Crown Copyright 1906"

Dr. Peter Stanier for kindly writing the foreword.

Bibliography

Quotes

D. M. Thomas 1971 The Puberty Tree: New and Selected Poems, Bloodaxe Books Ltd., 1992 page 49
W. Herbert Thomas 1893 Among Cornish Fisher Folk, Camborne 1898 page 157
John Wesley 1759 as quoted in The Trip to Far West, Smith, P. B., 1840 page 95
George Woodley Cornubia: A Poem in five cantos, Truro 1819 page 152

Penwith

Blight, J. T., A Week at the Land's End, Longman, London 1861
Carter, C., Cornish Shipwrecks, The North Coast Vol. 2, David & Charles, Newton Abbot 1970
Cooke, I., Journey to the Stones, Men-an-Tol Studio, 1987
Cornwall's Far West, Tor Mark Press Truro, 1969
Folliott-Stokes A. G., From St. Ives to Land's End, London 1908
Hannigan, D., Atlantic Edge, Penwith District Council 1995
Hudson W. H., The Land's End, Hutchinson and Co. 1908
Larn, R & B., Shipwrecks around Land's End, Tor Mark Press 1989
Noall, C., The Book of St. Ives 3rd impression, Baron Books Ltd. Buckingham 2000
Straffon, C., Ancient Sites in West Penwith, Meyn Mamvro Publications 1993
Payne, R., and Lewsey, L., The Romance of the Stones, Alexander Associates 1999
Weatherhill, C., Belerion, Ancient Sites of Land's End, Alison Hodge 1981

Cornwall and the South West

Baker, D. V., The Timeless Land, Adams & Dart, Bath 1973
Baker, D. V., The Spirit of Cornwall, W.H. Allen & Co. 1980
Bird, E., The Coasts of Cornwall, Alexander Associates, Fowey 1998
Bottrell, W., Traditions and Hearthside Stories of West Cornwall 2nd. series, Penzance 1873
Bottrell, W., Stories and Folk-lore of West Cornwall 3rd series, Penzance 1880
Folliott-Stokes A. G., The Cornish Coast and Moors, Plymouth 1928
Smith, B. P., The Trip to Far West, London Sherwood, Gilbert and Piper 1840
Stanier, P., South West Granite, Hillside St. Austell 1999
Stanier, P., The Work of Giants, St Ives Publishing Company 1988
Wood. W., The Strangers Hand-book to Cornwall, from Plymouth to Land's End, Devonport 1866

Mining

Brown, K., & Acton, B., Exploring Cornish Mines Vol. 1 Landfall Publications, Truro 1996
Noall, C., The St. Ives Mining District Vol. 2 Dyllansow, Truran Redruth 1993
Noall, C., The St. Just Mining District Vol. 2 D. Bradford Barton ltd., Truro 1973
Stanier, P., Cornwall's Mining Heritage, Twelveheads Press 1998

Cornish

Holmes, J., 1000 Cornish Place Names Explained, Truran 2000
Padel, O. J., Cornish Place Names, Alison Hodge 1988
Truran, C., A Short Cornish Dictionary Gerlyver Ber, Dyllansow Truran 2000

Guides

Cooke, I. Antiquities of West Cornwall, Guide One, The Men-an-Tol and nearby ancient sites, Men-an-Tol Studio 1990
Cooke, I. Antiquities of West Cornwall, Guide Four, The Tinner's Way, Men-an-Tol and nearby ancient sites, Studio 1991
Reid, N., Land's End Peninsula & The Tinner's Way, Friendly Guide, Cormorant Designs 1998

OCEAN

AT

Burthallan

lesveor Cliff

Old S

Spring

Spring

Higher Burthallan

Lower Burthallan

I V E S

Pedn-an-vounder